CONTENT

Warm up the motor and coast along with these fun and easy puzzles.

Start feeling the burn with these more challenging puzzles.

Take your puzzling power to another level with these ultra-intense brainteasers!

Get Ready for Fun and Games!

Look no further, kids! *Brain Games™ Kids: Puzzle Crazy!* is here, and it's jam-packed with brainteasers that will pump up your puzzle power and provide loads of fun. You'll find twisty mazes, dot-to-dots, illustrated puzzles, word challenges, and many more.

We've put our heads together to come up with a big-time collection of puzzles and loaded them into this handy pocket-size book. Your favorite brain builders are sorted into levels, so you can kick off with an easy one in the first level or fast-track straight to the toughest challenges in Level 3. Skip around and work a variety of puzzles—you'll have fun for days, and your mind will get the workout it needs!

BRAIN GAMES™ kids

PUZZLE CRAZY!

Publications International, Ltd.

Puzzle Constructors: Cihan Altay, Ryan Browne, Keith Burns, Clarity Media Ltd., Jeff Cockrell, Julie K. Cohen, Garry Colby, Conceptis Puzzles, Don Cook, Sean Dove, Harvey Estes, The Grabarchuk Family, Peter Grosshauser, David Helton, Naomi Lipsky, Janet McDonnell, Emily Rice, Pete Sarjeant, Andy Scordellis, Lauren Anne Sharp, Terry Stickels, Jen Torche, Wayne Robert Williams, Alex Willmore

Illustrators: Chris Gattorna, Jen Torche

Cover Puzzles: Cihan Altay, The Grabarchuk Family

Another helpful thing is that every answer is included in the back of the book. You want to be sure to give each puzzle a try, but the solutions are there to get you back on track in case you get stuck.

Kids, now you're ready to get moving! So grab a pencil, and get your noggin cooking with *Brain Games™ Kids: Puzzle Crazy!*

Parent's note: The more than 115 kid-friendly brainteasers in *Brain Games™ Kids: Puzzle Power!* will hold your child's interest for hours while also giving their brains a boost and improving their language skills, analytic thinking, and logical reasoning.

Compact and portable, your youngsters can tote this mobile book everywhere they go—school, dance class, soccer practice, or a visit to the dentist's office. (It might even make the trip to a teeth scrubbing a little more fun!) So give them this book, and turn them loose on puzzling!

GET YOUR MIND GOING
Giraffe

Can you find your way from head to tail through this long-necked giraffe?

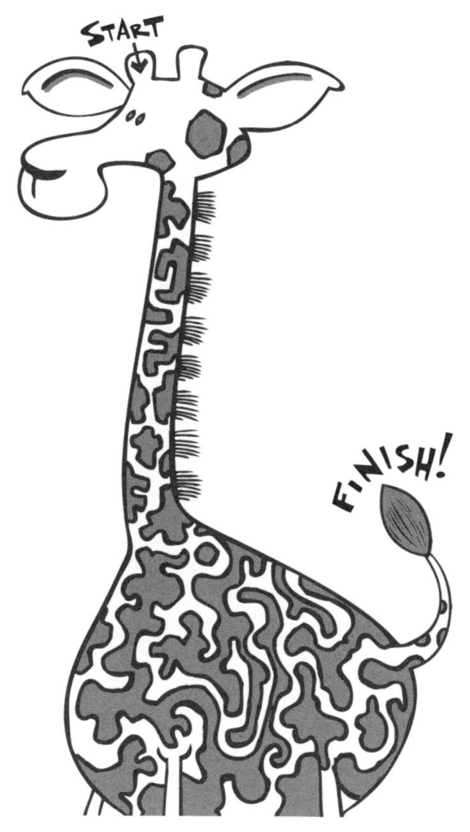

Answer on page 128.

Fetch!

Find the 10 differences in these 2 pictures.

7   Answers on page 128.

Pic-doku

The grid below is divided into 4 sections. Your job is to have each of the 4 animals appear once in each section and in each row and column. Fill each square with the animal's image or the letter that represents it. No animal can repeat in any section, row, or column.

   Answer on page 128.

Rhyme Time

Each clue leads to a 2-word answer that rhymes, such as BIG PIG or STABLE TABLE. The numbers in parentheses after the clue give the number of letters in each word. For example, "cookware taken from the oven (3, 3)" would be "hot pot."

1. Jelly made from shell-covered sea creatures (4, 3):

   ____

2. Mud-colored dress (5, 4): _______________

3. Location for a speedy competition (4, 5):

   ____

4. Robbery of a 10-cent coin (4, 5): _______________

5. Long-winded talk on the sand (5, 6): _______________

6. Soggy dog or cat (3, 3): _______________

7. Rule prohibiting tin containers (3, 3):

   ____

8. Tidy roadway (4, 6):

   ____

    Answers on page 128.

Hen Party

Which figure is the mirror image of the one in the box?

A.

B.

C.

Answer on page 128.

Have Your Cake

Of the ingredients below, which 2 would **not** be used when baking a cake?

     Answers on page 128.

Fit It

Name each of the animals below, then fit those names into the crossword grid on the next page.

ACROSS

DOWN

Answers on page 128.

After Practice

Find 8 common objects listed below hidden in the picture.

DISC

DOUGHNUT

FEATHER

FLASHLIGHT

LADLE

RULER

THUMBTACK

WRISTWATCH

    Answers on page 129.

Flower Growth

Which of these flowers has the longest stem?

Answer on page 129.

Dinner Party

Someone's jumbled up this dinner party! Can you help set things right by finding all 9 differences?

      Answers on page 129.

Face Off

Can you spot the 2 identical faces?

     Answer on page 129.

Paper Fold

What animal's name is written on this folded paper?

Word Ladder

Can you change just one letter on each line to transform the top word to the bottom word? Don't change the order of the letters, and make sure you have a common English word at each step.

LID

______

______

TOP

Answers on page 129.

Stop Signs

A heavy sign recently fell on our sign painter's head, and since then he has mixed up a few stop signs. Help him sort out his mistakes by finding the 3 pairs of signs that match.

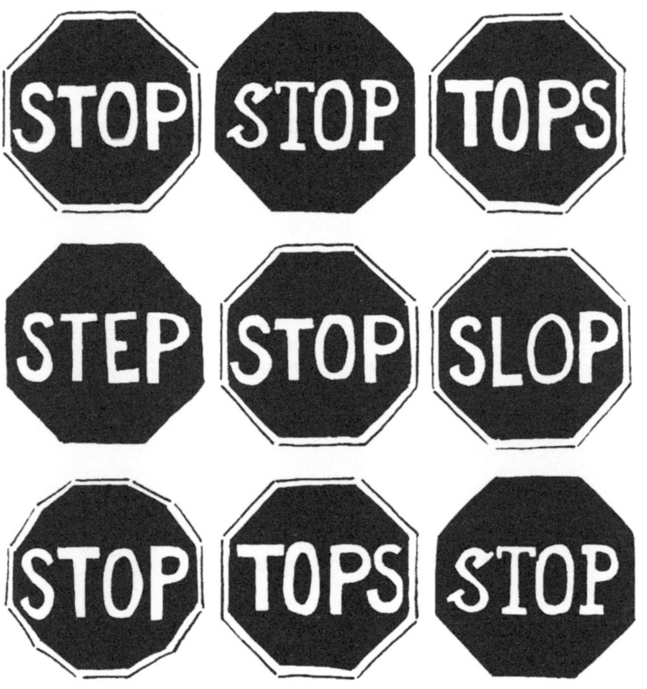

     Answers on page 129.

Toy Box

Match each toy to its silhouette.

 Answers on page 130.

At the Zoo

Every word listed is contained within the group of letters below. Words can be found in a straight line, horizontally, vertically, or diagonally. They may be read either forward or backward.

```
B  J  Z  E  B  R  A  S  K  T  W
B  A  T  S  L  Y  D  R  N  E  L
R  J  M  L  Z  R  K  A  S  F  L
T  A  A  O  A  M  H  N  E  F  R
N  M  G  Z  N  P  K  X  K  A  X
A  T  I  U  E  K  P  M  A  R  C
M  L  H  L  O  X  E  P  N  I  H
M  K  E  Y  R  C  R  Y  S  G  I
Y  W  A  L  L  I  R  O  G  L  M
L  R  N  M  H  Z  N  L  F  K  P
R  J  V  R  E  G  I  T  N  K  H
```

BATS	GIRAFFE	MONKEY
CHIMP	GORILLA	SNAKES
COUGAR	LIZARDS	TIGER
ELEPHANT	LLAMA	ZEBRA

     Answers on page 130.

Find the Blocks:

Find the shape below in the grid as many times as listed. Shapes cannot be flipped or turned.

x3

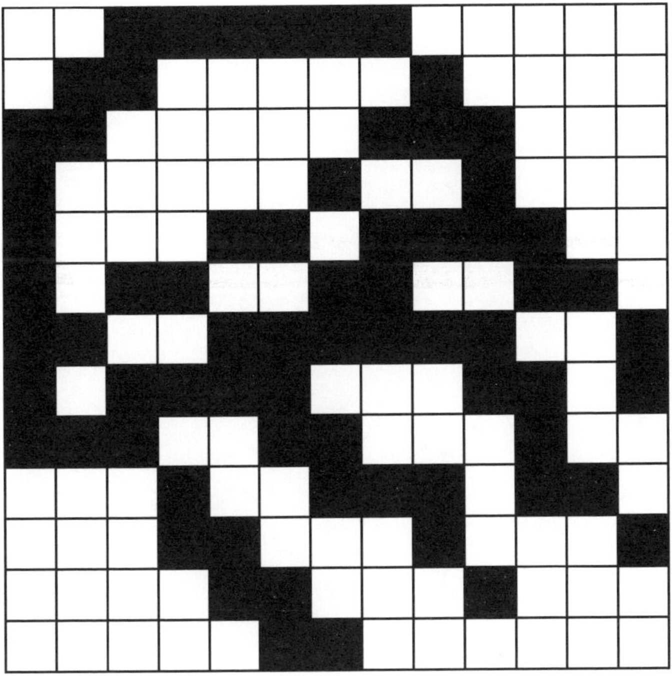

Answers on page 130.

1-2-3

Place the number 1, 2, or 3 in each empty circle. The challenge is to have only these 3 numbers in each connected row and column—no number should repeat. Any combination is allowed.

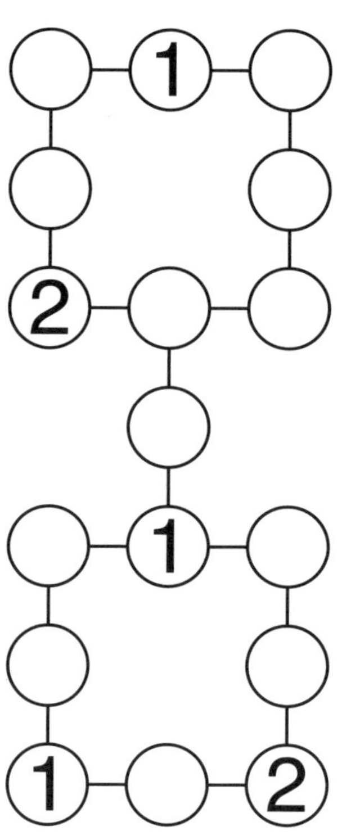

Answer on page 130.

Egg Hunt

There are 10 dinosaur eggs hidden in this prehistoric scene. Can you find them all?

25   Answers on page 130.

Family Ties

Divide the grid into 9 sections with each section containing 4 squares. Every section must contain one of each of the family members—mother, father, brother, and sister.

Hint: Look for places where the same family member is bunched together, and start there.

Answer on page 130.

Hungry Fox

Help this little desert fox find his way into the burrow.

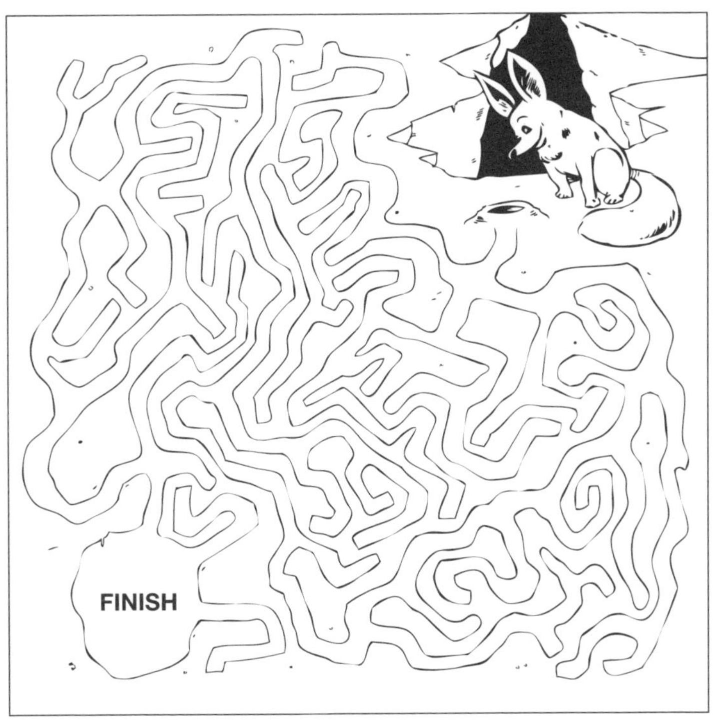

Answer on page 131.

Combo Crossword

Half of the clues in this puzzle are pictures, and the other half define words that you have to figure out. When you are sure of a word, write it in the grid going either across or down.

ACROSS

1. 

4. 

6. 

7. 

8. 

9. 

11. 

13. 

15. 

16. 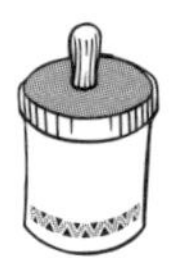

DOWN

1. The man married to Mom (rhymes with HOP)
2. A performer like Denzel Washington
3. Opposite of west
4. "Beauty and _____ Beast"
5. You write on this material
8. A baby will _____ on the floor (rhymes with DRAWL)
9. _____ for joy (rhymes with PUMPS)
10. A ginger _____ is a kind of cookie
12. Roses are _____, violets are blue
14. This dessert has a crust

Answers on page 131.

Space Case

Can you get Spaceman Stan through the cosmos and back to his rocket ship?

Answer on page 131.

Wagon Ride

Which figure is the mirror image of the one in the box?

 Answer on page 131.

Math

Every word listed is contained within the group of letters on the next page. Words can be found in a straight line horizontally, vertically, or diagonally. They may be read either forward or backward.

ADD

AVERAGE

CALCULATOR

COUNT

DECIMAL

DIGITS

DIVIDE

EQUALS SIGN

EQUATION

FIGURE

FRACTION

MATHEMATICS

MINUS

MULTIPLY

NUMBERS

PLUS

SUBTRACT

SUMS

TALLY

TIMES

TOTAL

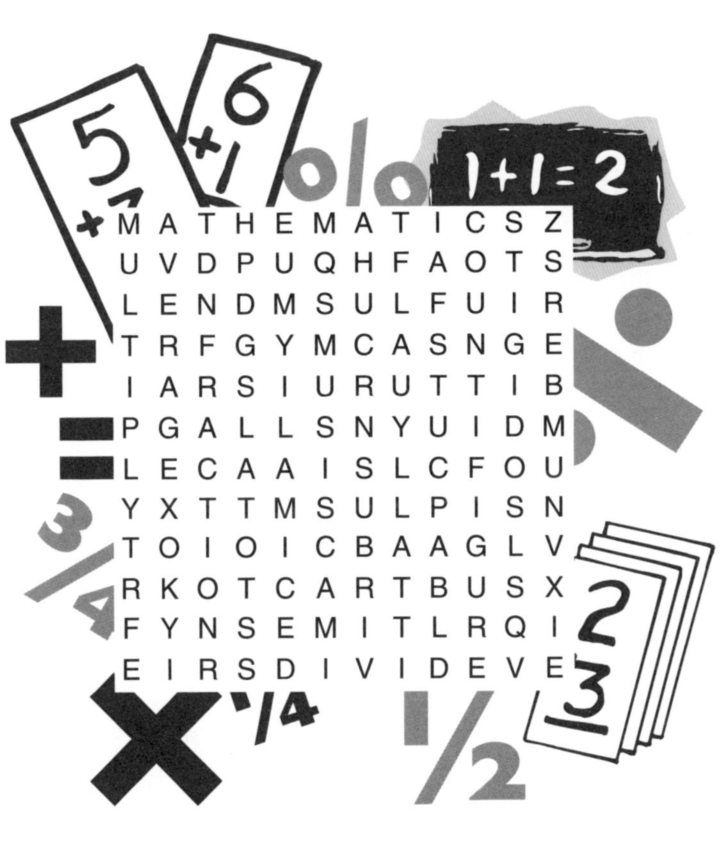

Answers on page 131.

It's Magic

There are 10 differences between these 2 magical illustrations. Can you find them all?

 Answers on page 131.

Decoder

Use the code below to reveal the answer to this riddle:
What is a train's favorite song?

A =   B =   C =   D =   E =

F =   G =   H =   I =   J =

K =   L =   M =   N =   O =

P =   Q =   R =   S =   T =

U =   V =   W =   X =   Y =

Z =

__ __ __ __ __ __ __ __ __ __ __ __ __ __ __!

     Answer on page 131.

Staircase Crossword

Use the pictures to help you fill in the puzzle. The words go down and then across.

DOWN

1.

3.

5.

ACROSS

2.
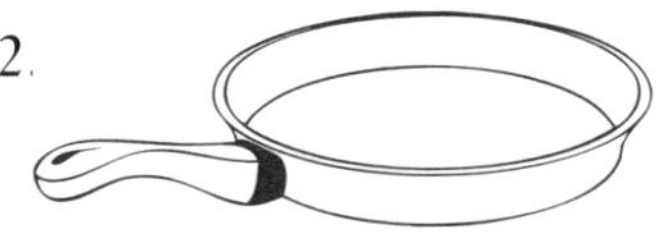

4.

6.

Answers on page 132.

W Is for Witch

In this picture, there are 10 things beginning with the letter **W**. Can you find them all?

Answers on page 132.

Flippy Numbers

Below is an incorrect equation. Can you swap 2 of the number cards to get a correct equation?

$$8 + 7 + 6 = 5 + 10$$

Chain Words

Place 2 letters in the middle squares that will complete one word and start another. For example, ER would complete FLI - ER - ROR.

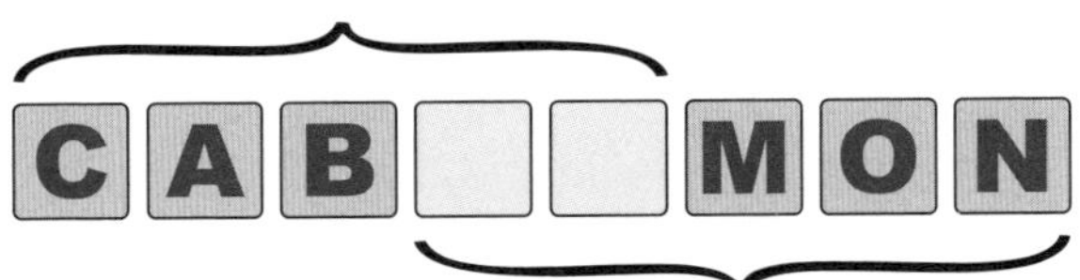

39   Answers on page 132.

Pic-doku

The grid below is divided into 4 sections. Your job is to have each of the 4 fruits appear once in each section and in each row and column. Fill each square with the fruit's image or the letter that represents it. No fruit can repeat in any section, row, or column.

     Answer on page 132.

Find the Blocks

Find the shape below in the grid as many times as listed. Shapes cannot be flipped or turned.

 x5

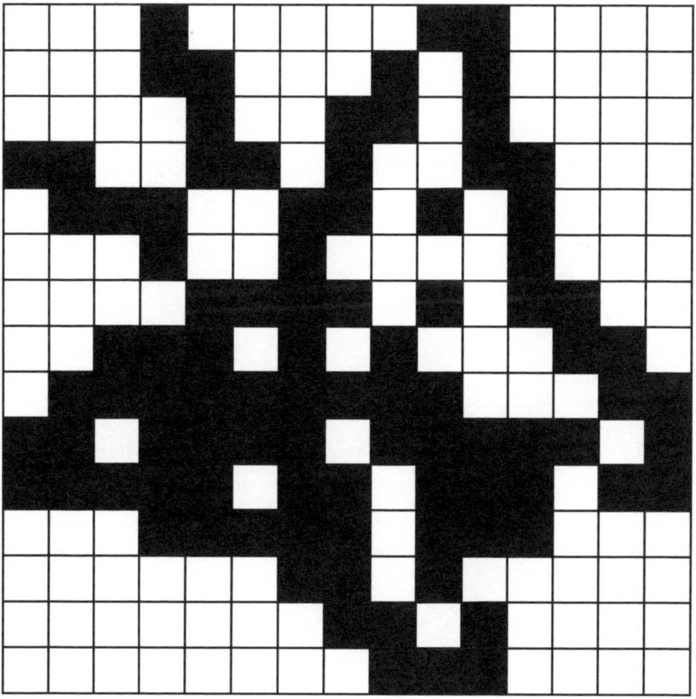

 Answers on page 132.

Snow Day

Which figure is the mirror image of the one in the box?

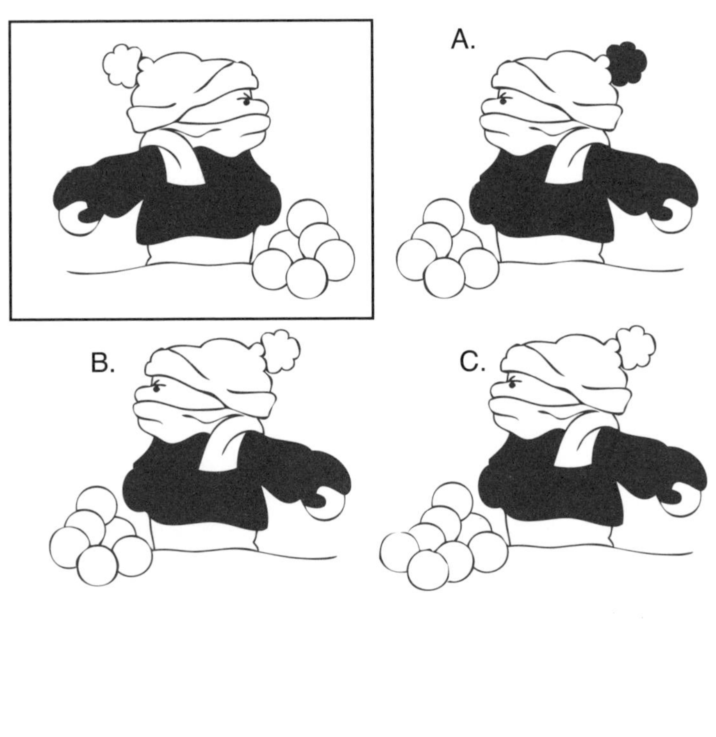

42   Answer on page 132.

Wood Floor

Scurry across the floorboards to help this mouse find his way home!

Answer on page 133.

Anagrammar

There are 2 words on this torn parchment that are anagrams (rearrangements of the same letters) of each other. Trace the lines connecting the circles to find out what the second word is.

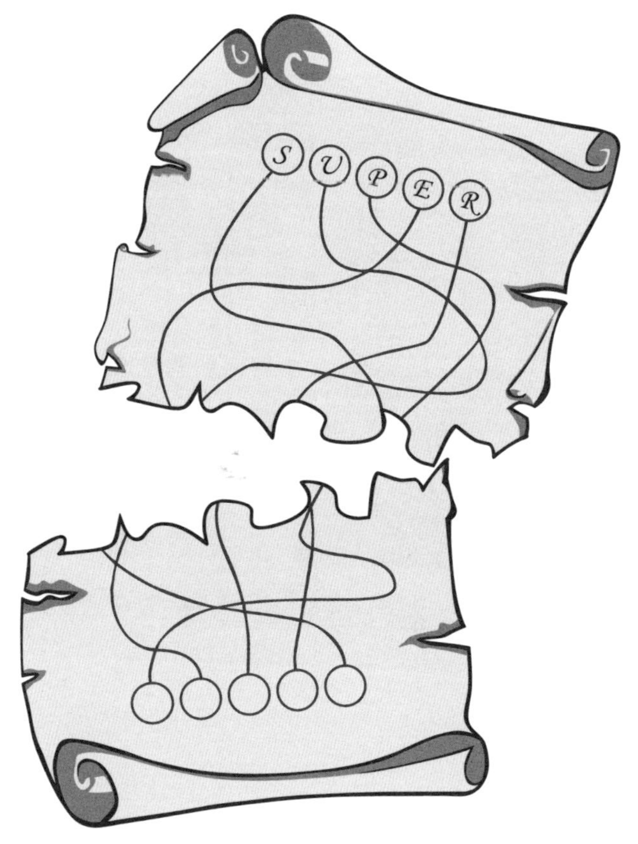

44

Answer on page 133.

Green Thumb

Help the gardener find her way out of this flowering maze.

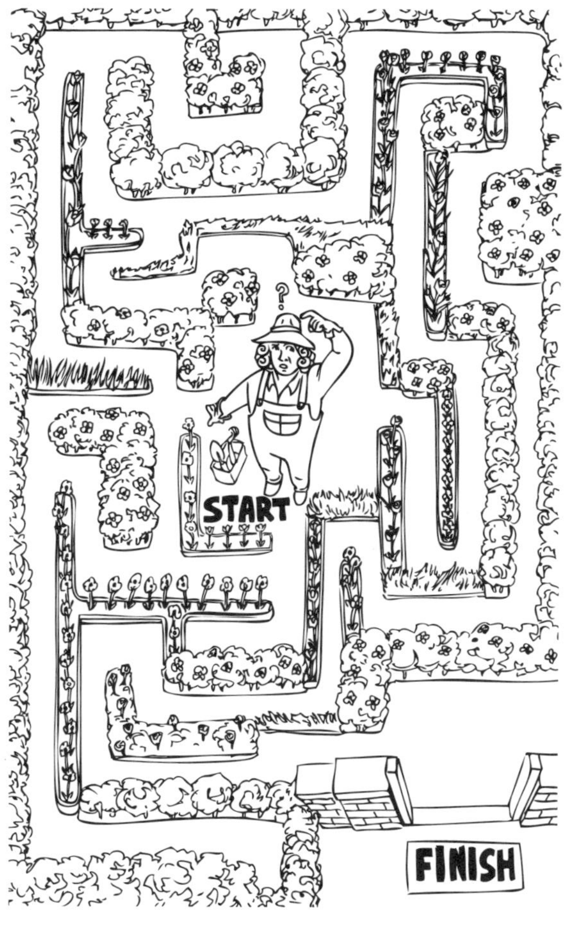

Answer on page 133.

Boot Shopping

Howdy partner! Can you help Cowboy Kyle find the one pair of matching boots?

     Answer on page 133.

Dog Walker

Looks like Annie has a tangled mess on her hands! Can you follow the path of each leash to see which dog it is attached to?

Answers on page 133.

EXERCISE YOUR BRAIN
Insects

Every word listed is contained within the group of letters on the next page. Words can be found in a straight line horizontally, vertically, or diagonally. They may be read either forward or backward.

ANTS

BEETLE

BUMBLEBEE

CATERPILLAR

COCKROACH

DRAGONFLY

EARWIG

FIREFLY

FLIES

HORNET

LADYBUG

LICE

LOCUST

MAYFLY

MOSQUITO

MOTH

WASP

L K C N X I T S E R T S C
S L X A M O S Q U I T O O
T R R Y T M D K Z D K T C
N Y F L O E E T R P E V K
A L L T A L R A F N G T R
M I H F T D G P R C S F O
K C L E E O Y O I U E Z A
T E E X N R H B C L I Z C
H B M F M P I O U T L Y H
N N L L M Y L F T G F A R
P Y C G V D G I W R A E R
T P S A W N R M A Y F L Y
B U M B L E B E E M V N H

Answers on page 134.

Row Your Boat

Something's fishy between these 2 scenes. Can you spot all 6 changes?

Answers on page 134.

Ribbit

Which lucky frog just caught lunch?

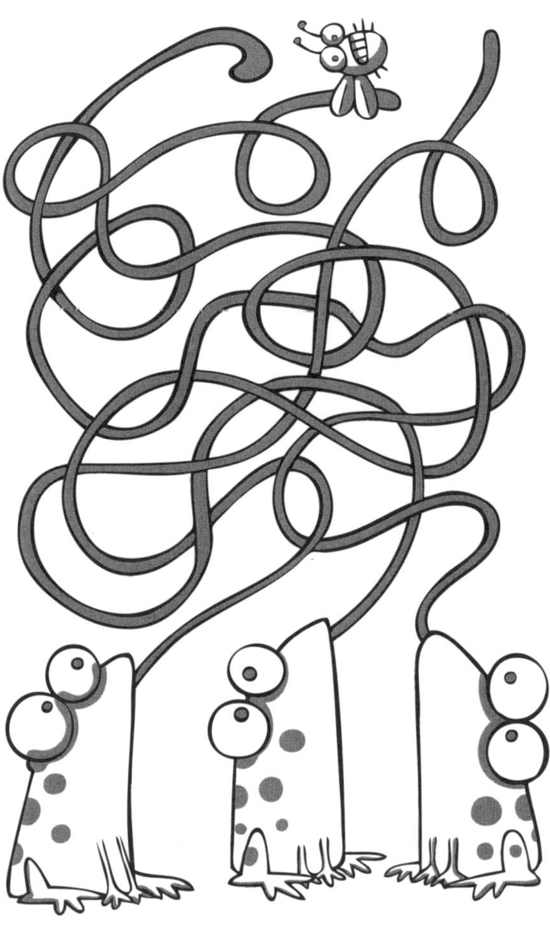

Answers on page 134.

Flower Growth

Which of these flowers has the longest stem?

 Answer on page 134.

Squid on the High Seas

Something sure seems fishy when looking at these 2 illustrations. Can you "sea" all 8 differences?

55 Answers on page 134.

Picture Rhymes

Each object on the left rhymes with one object on the right. When you find the rhyming pair, draw a line to connect them! We did the first one for you.

 Answers on page 134.

Night Light

Which figure is the mirror image of the one in the box?

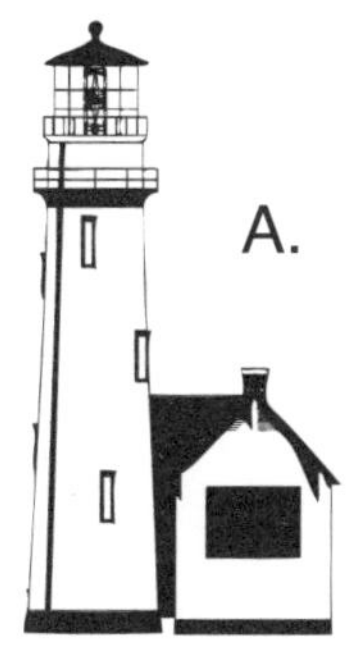

A.

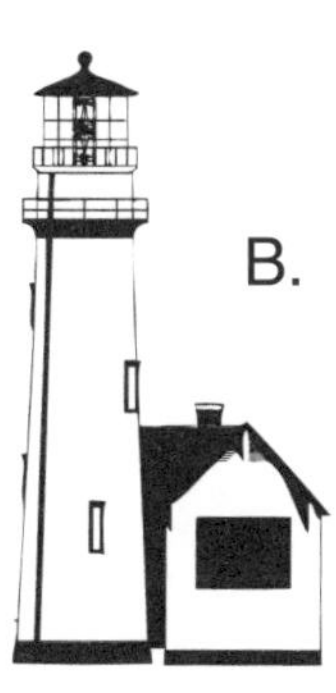

B.

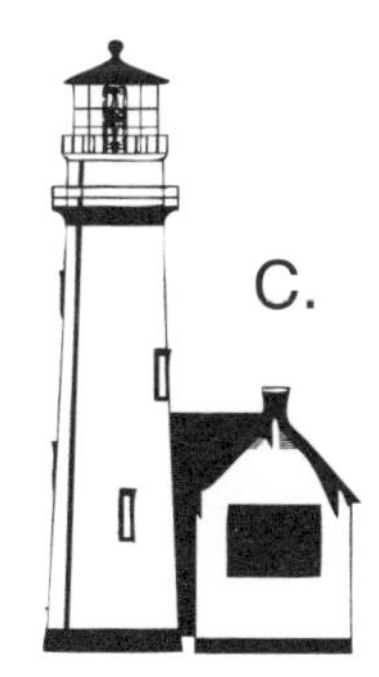

C.

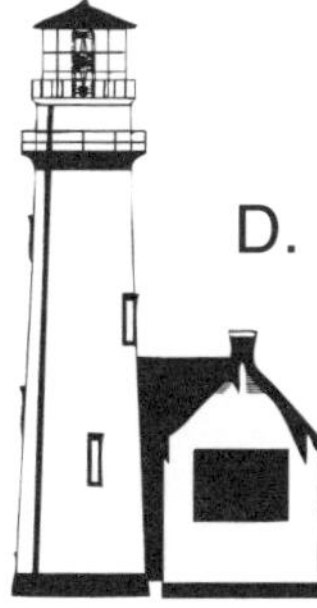

D.

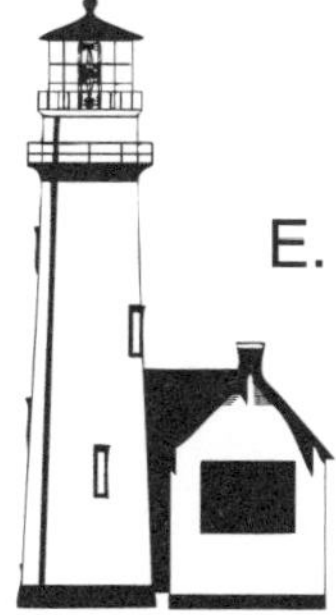

E.

 Answer on page 135.

M Is for Marbles

Can you find all 9 things beginning with the letter **M** in this picture?

Answers on page 135.

Zoo

Can you find the names of all 6 animals pictured below hidden in the grid? Words can be found in a straight line horizontally, vertically, or diagonally. They may read either forward or backward.

     Answers on page 135.

Face Off

Can you spot the 2 identical faces?

       Answer on page 135.

Dog Maze

Help this little pup find its way to a juicy bone!

Answer on page 135.

Letters on the Move

Rearrange the letters to make 2 new words. Use the pictures to help!

otp _ _ _   _ _ _

eap _ _ _   _ _ _

tras _ _ _ _   _ _ _ _

stac _ _ _ _   _ _ _ _

ent _ _ _   _ _ _

plis _ _ _ _   _ _ _ _

malp _ _ _ _   _ _ _ _

linas _ _ _ _ _   _ _ _ _ _

Answers on page 135.

Find the Blocks

Find the shapes below in the grid as many times as listed. Shapes cannot be flipped or turned.

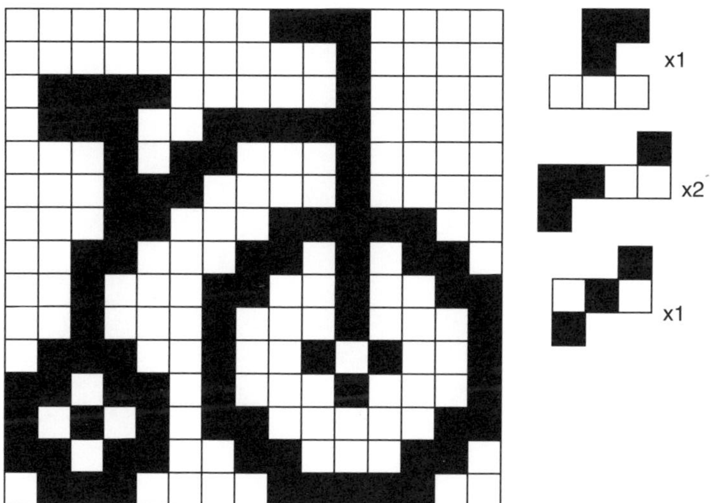

63   Answers on page 136.

Picture-by-Number

Shade in the numbers that are divisible by 2. Once complete, you will reveal a simple image.

13	75	63	29	31	35	63
74	96	9	21	65	76	34
26	90	37	53	29	90	22
87	65	99	40	9	65	13
23	29	77	49	63	71	29
40	26	79	55	93	2	98
79	91	78	42	34	35	85

Answer on page 136.

Tundra of T's

There are a ton of things beginning with the letter **T** in this image. If you find 10, that would be terrific! Find 16, and you have this puzzle solved to a T!

Answers on page 136.

Rhyme Time

Each clue leads to a 2-word answer that rhymes, such as BIG PIG or STABLE TABLE. The numbers in parentheses after the clue give the number of letters in each word. For example, "cookware taken from the oven (3, 3)" would be "hot pot."

1. The strength of one's chomp (4, 5): _________________

2. Food for the moo crew (3, 4): _________________

3. Communication device attached to a king's chair (6, 5): _________________

4. Wealthy broom-rider (4, 5): _________________

5. Downpour of iguanas and chameleons (6, 8):

   ____

6. Squashed baseball cap (4, 3): _________________

7. Chill cheddar (6, 6): _________________

8. Lunar melody (4, 4): _________________

9. Public play area with lots of trees but no lights (4, 4):

   ____

10. Chocolate bars dropped on the beach (5, 5):

    ____

    Answers on page 136.

Polly Pirate

Complete this illustration by drawing the missing pieces.
Each missing piece is a copy of its opposite side.

 Answer on page 136.

State Your Name

ACROSS

1. Put 2 and 2 together
4. Really strange
7. Ballplayer's hat
10. Feel sorry (sounds like 11-Across)
11. Pal of Pooh
12. Serious poem
13. State that borders 33-Across
16. Deer guy
17. Did a burglar's work
18. Figured out
20. Used a bench
21. Girl's name (hidden in "denial")
23. Perform in plays
26. Boy's name (hidden in "delivery")
28. Land divisions
30. Ginger _____ (soft drinks)
33. Smallest state in the USA: 2 wds.
36. Cut the grass
37. Inquire
38. Road topper
39. Tiny Tim, to Bob Cratchit
40. Tub with a whirlpool
41. Secret agent

DOWN

1. Circle section
2. Twosomes
3. Minor car accident result
4. West Coast state
5. One of the Seven Dwarfs
6. Marks over j and i
7. Hot chocolate drink
8. Grownup
9. Boy's name (hidden in "competence")
14. Pester
15. "_____ not fair!"
19. Final score without losers
22. State next to Canada
23. Sneeze sound
24. It's on a king's head
25. Boy's name (hidden in "private detective")

27. Sick
28. They're in your sleeves
29. Large bodies of water
31. Has dinner, for example
32. Ginger cookie
34. Online company (hidden in "crispy")
35. What socks do on a clothesline

Anagrammar

There are 2 words on this torn parchment that are anagrams (rearrangements of the same letters) of each other. Trace the lines connecting the circles to find out what the second word is.

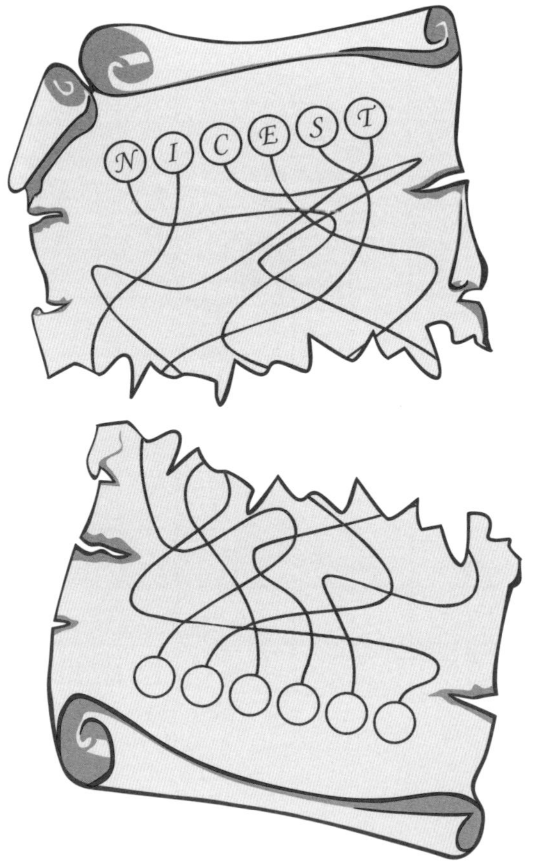

70 Answer on page 136.

Black Hole

Ready to explore the mysteries of the universe? Take a journey through space and time as you travel through this maze!

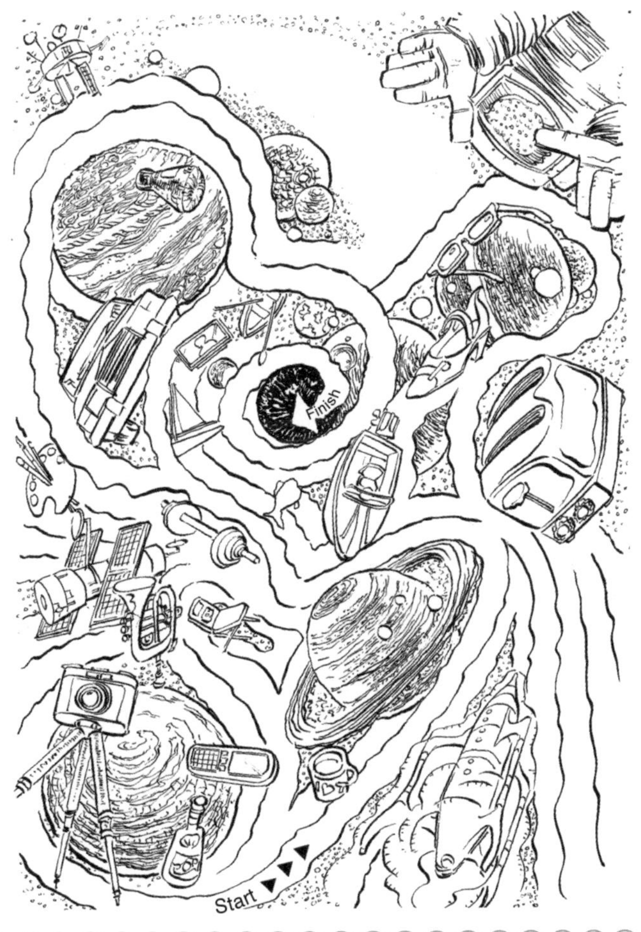

Answer on page 137.

Sea World!

It should be a splash to find all 9 differences in these images!

   Answers on page 137.

Pic-doku

The grid below is divided into 4 sections. Your job is to have each of the 4 pieces of furniture appear once in each section and in each row and column. Fill each square with the furniture's image or the letter that represents it. No item can repeat in any section, row, or column.

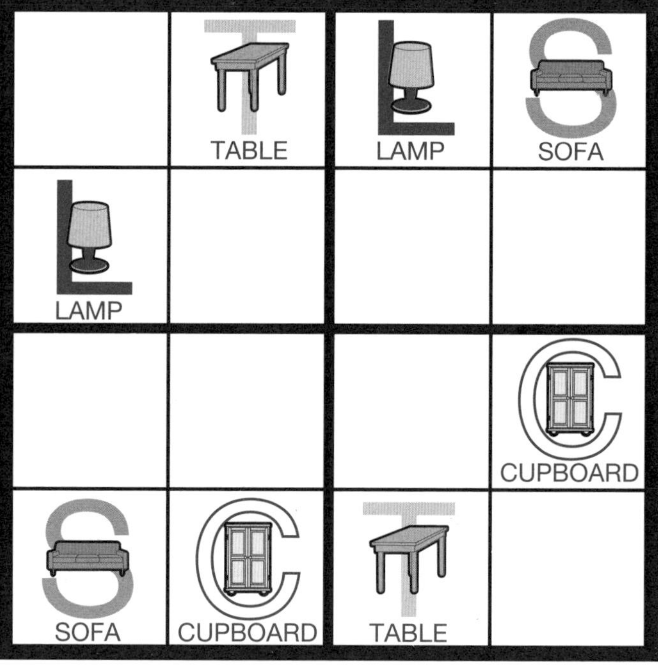

 Answer on page 137.

Rhyme Time

Each clue leads to a 2-word answer that rhymes, such as BIG PIG or STABLE TABLE. The numbers in parentheses after the clue give the number of letters in each word. For example, "cookware taken from the oven (3, 3)" would be "hot pot."

1. Secret agent, after toweling off (3, 3): _______________

2. Container for insects (3, 3): _______________

3. Sofa for a grumpy person (6, 5): _______________

4. King's cruel wife (4, 5): _______________

5. Regulation enforced by lifeguards (4, 4): _______________

6. Sky-colored footwear (4, 4): _______________

7. Mickey's mansion (5, 5): _______________

8. Angry boy (3, 3): _______________

75   Answers on page 137.

Family Ties

Divide the grid into 9 sections with each section containing 4 squares. Every section must contain one of each of the family members—mother, father, brother, and sister.

Hint: Look for places where the same family member is bunched together, and start there.

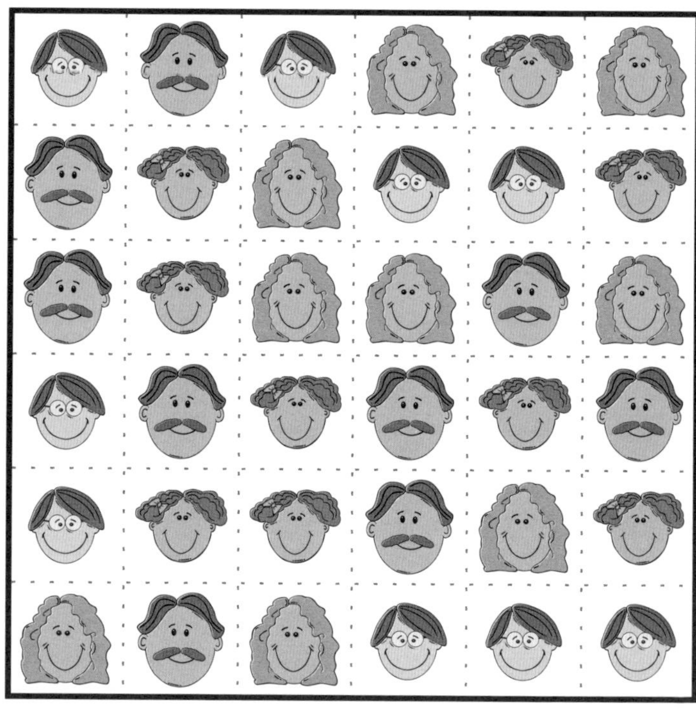

Answer on page 137.

Polar-mobile

Looks like this polar bear is in a hurry! Guide him safely through the snow to get him home.

 Answer on page 137.

Face Off

Can you spot the 2 identical faces?

Answer on page 137.

Dot-to-Dot

Draw a line from consecutive numbers, starting at 1 and ending at 63, to reveal a leggy underwater creature.

Answer on page 138.

Art Class

Find the 10 objects listed below hidden in the picture.

BANANA	RING	SPATULA
CUP	RULER	WORM
ENVELOPE	SAILBOAT	
FRIED EGG	SOCK	

Answers on page 138.

Paper Fold

What vegetable's name is written on this folded paper?

Chain Words

Place 3 letters in the middle squares that will complete one word and start another. For example, TAR would complete GUI - TAR - GET.

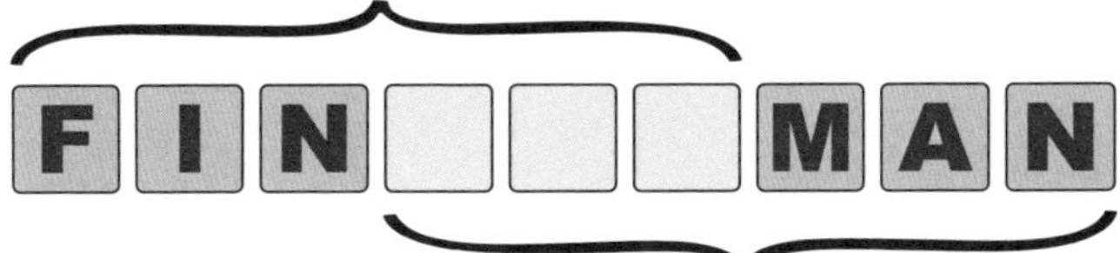

81　　　Answers on page 138.

Tricky Tomb

Search for the lost tomb in this creepy maze, but be careful; you don't want to end up in a mummy's grip!

 Answer on page 138.

Flower Growth

Which of these flowers has the longest stem?

 Answer on page 138.

Robo Repair

Fill in the missing pieces of the robot by drawing the silhouettes on its body.

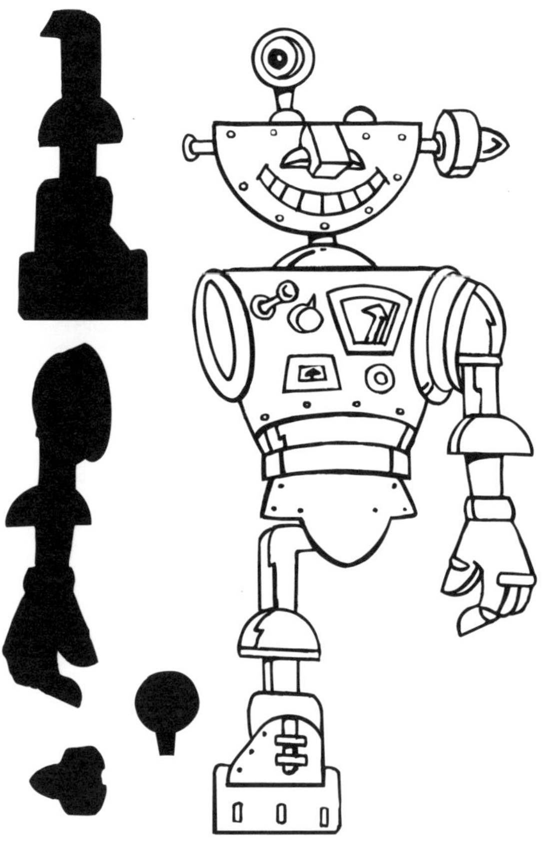

Answer on page 138.

Farm Fiasco

The farm animals have run amok! Can you find all 10 problems in this picture and set things right?

 Answers on page 138.

Boo!

These kids are dressed up and ready for a night of candy! See if you can find each of the 6 costumes in the grid.

A Rose Is a Rose

Which figure is the mirror image of the one in the box?

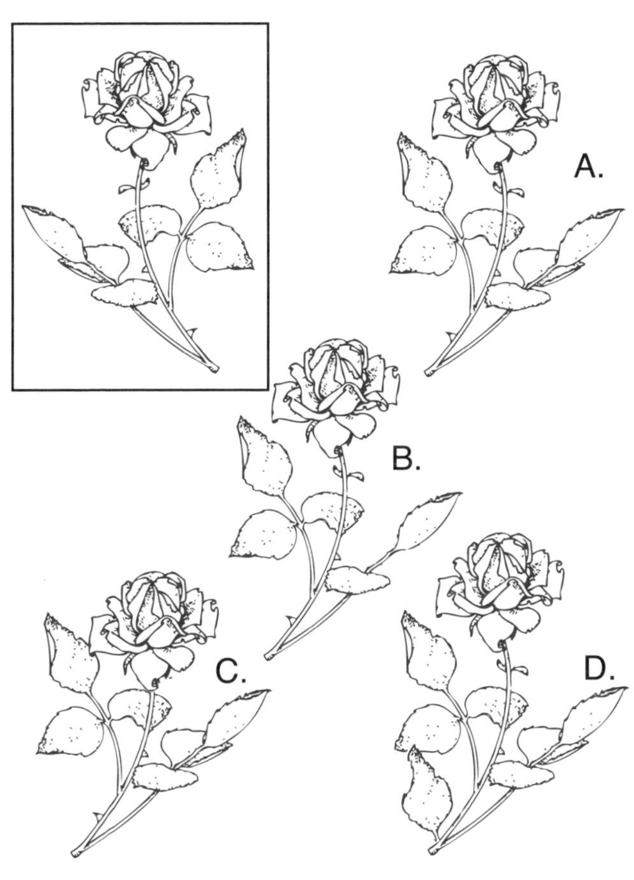

Answer on page 139.

TURN THE HEAT UP
Fruit Bowl

Find your way through the maze to make your escape!

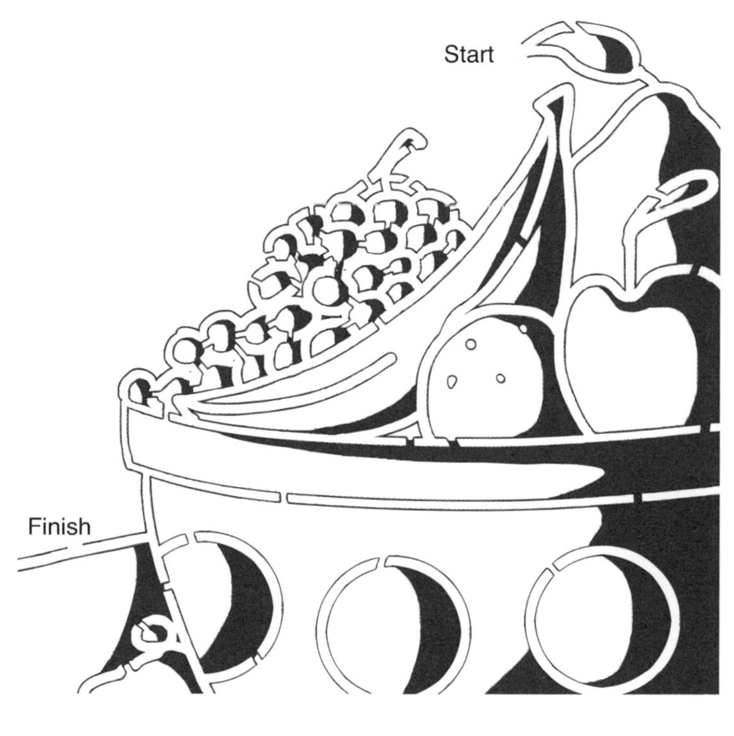

 Answer on page 139.

Airport

Can you find all 10 problems with this picture before you take off?

Answers on page 139.

Birds of a Feather

ACROSS

1. Used a chair
4. TV show: "My Name Is _____"
8. Boy's name (hidden in "not to worry")
9. It holds a model airplane together
10. White wading bird
11. Bird with blue eggs
12. Memorable time in history
13. Cheer at a bullfight
15. Game with "Reverse" cards
16. Door openers
18. Eve's husband
20. Bird with a curved neck
22. Kind of carpet
23. "Of _____ I sing"
27. Prefix for angle or pod
29. It'll float your boat
31. Raw metal
32. Bird that is a symbol of America
34. Small game bird
36. Sound in a canyon
37. Encourage
38. Home for a bird
39. "…have you _____ wool?"

DOWN

1. Runaway cat
2. Had a meal
3. Dog in "The Wizard of Oz"
4. "I'm better than you" feeling
5. Book of photographs
6. Complete wreck
7. Jay of late-night TV
8. Shrek, for one
10. Scream in the comic strips
11. Make over
14. Big
17. "Quiet, please!"
19. Bug that lives on a hill
21. Freedom from hardship
22. Breathes out rather loudly
24. Big sandwich
25. One of the Great Lakes

26. Fish without fins
27. What a 12-year-old becomes after a year
28. 100-yard dash, for example
30. Shade of blue
33. Land around a house
35. Large coffee container

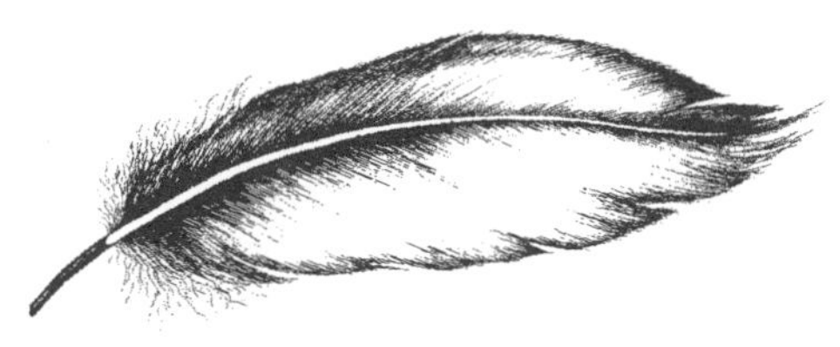

Answers on page 139.

Plenty of P's

Can you pick out all the printed possessions that begin with the letter **P?** Finding 18 would be pretty good; finding 23 would be perfect!

 Answers on page 140.

Go Fish

How many different kinds of fish do you see here? Are there more striped or polka-dotted fish? There is only 1 of which kind of fish?

 Answers on page 140.

Rhyme Time

Each clue leads to a 2-word answer that rhymes, such as RED BED or LARGE BARGE. The numbers in parentheses after the clue give the number of letters in each word. For example, "cookware taken from the oven (3, 3)" would be "hot pot."

1. A portly porker (3, 3): _______________

2. A pickup stranded in the snow (5, 5): _______________

3. Wed Harold (5, 5): _______________

4. Excellent fishing lure (5, 4): _______________

5. A bee attack, sometime between winter and summer (6, 5): _______________

6. Serious slumber (4, 5): _______________

7. Evaluator of the king's comedian (6, 6): _______________

8. Purple flyboy (6, 5): _______________

9. Friendly rodents (4, 4): _______________

10. Pale hero dressed in armor (5, 6): _______________

11. Sturdy piece of kitchen furniture (6, 5):

____

12. Select footwear (6, 5): _______________

13. Thief who preys on libraries (4, 5): _______________

14. Lengthy tune (4, 4): _______________

15. Pleasant jog or sprint (3, 3): _______________

16. Eat potato chips plain (4, 3): _______________

17. What she does by the seashore (5, 6): _______________

      Answers on page 140.

Word Ladder

Can you change just one letter on each line to transform the top word to the bottom word? Don't change the order of the letters, and make sure you have a common English word at each step.

WARM

_____

_____

_____

_____

COOL

Paper Fold

What word is written on this folded paper?

96 Answers on page 140.

Fanfare

Which figure is the mirror image of the one in the box?

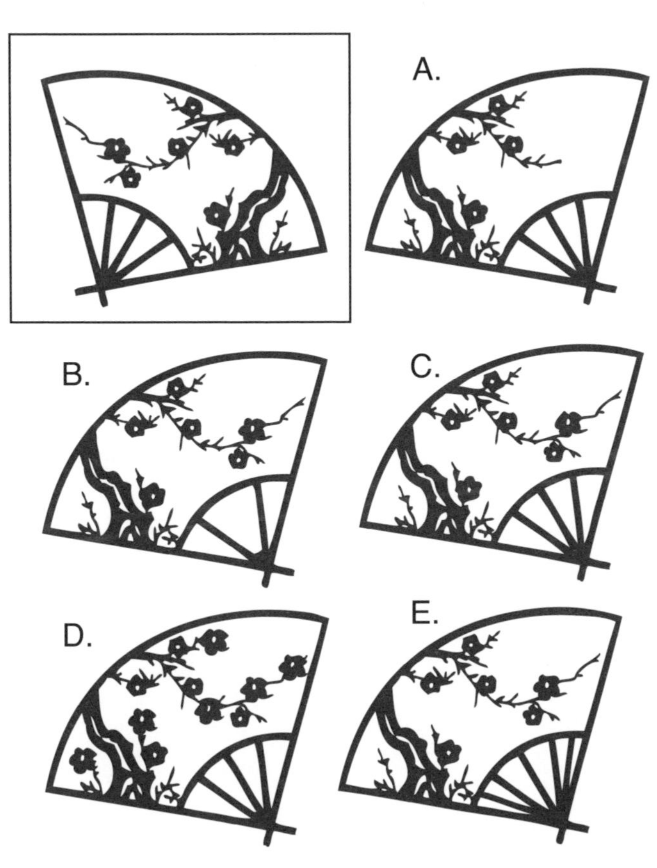

     Answer on page 140.

Pic-doku

The grid below is divided into 4 sections. Your job is to have each of the 4 pieces of furniture appear once in each section and in each row and column. Fill each square with the furniture's image or the letter that represents it. No item can repeat in any section, row, or column.

          Answer on page 140.

Monkeying Around

Help this monkey find his way through the bamboo maze to the banana treat at the end.

Answer on page 141.

Find the Blocks

Find the shapes below in the grid as many times as listed. Shapes cannot be flipped or turned.

   Answers on page 141.

Tangle

Several puzzle pieces have been laid on the table, one by one. Which one is on the bottom of the pile?

Answer on page 141.

Fruit and Vegetable Stand

Something's not ripe with these 2 illustrations—can you spot the 8 differences?

Answers on page 141.

Corral the Cows

Can you help the cowboy reach the herd?

Answer on page 141.

Family Ties

Divide the grid into 9 sections with each section containing 4 squares. Every section must contain one of each of the family members—mother, father, brother, and sister.

Hint: Look for places where the same family member is bunched together, and start there.

   Answer on page 141.

Picture-by-Number

Shade in the numbers that are divisible by 3. Once complete, a simple image will be revealed.

24	55	52	21	37	17	60
63	39	94	33	61	42	54
13	94	96	48	18	20	53
33	72	99	87	60	45	21
14	23	6	72	27	89	67
11	72	94	78	67	72	59
15	39	8	96	35	3	66

Answer on page 142.

Jetpack!

Follow the trails of smoke to reach the jetpack flyer before he zips away!

Answer on page 142.

Pic-doku

The grid below is divided into 4 sections. Your job is to have each of the 4 fruits appear once in each section and in each row and column. Fill each square with the fruit's image or the letter that represents it. No item can repeat in any section, row, or column.

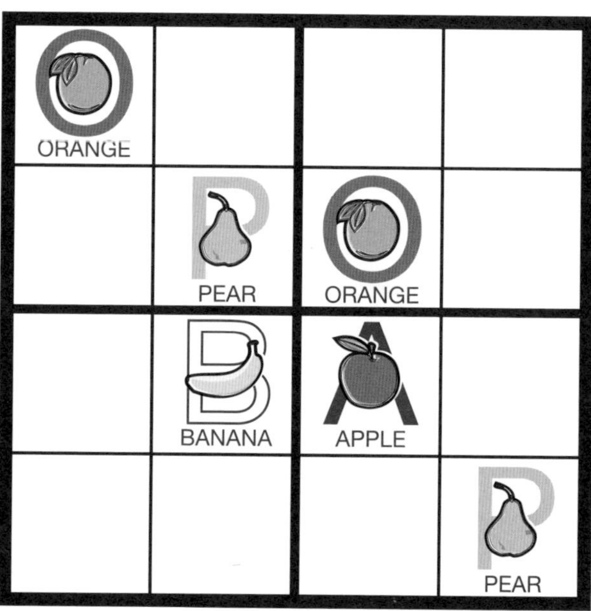

     Answer on page 142.

Recycling Day

Find the 9 hidden objects listed below in the illustration.

BANANA	PENNANT
BUTTON	SAILBOAT
ENVELOPE	TEACUP
GOLF CLUB	TOOTHBRUSH
PENCIL	

   Answers on page 142.

Riddle Scramble

Use the clues below to help unscramble the words on the next page. Once you've done that, unscramble the letters found in the boxes to solve this riddle: I'm drafty and the center of many fairy tales. What am I?

1. Rapunzel let her hair down from high inside a ______.

2. I'm surrounded by water called a ______.

3. Camelot, Sherwood Forest, and I are found in this country.

4. At night, I close these to keep out outlaws and invaders.

5. I'm made of this hard material that has to be chiseled.

6. This is where many people go to pray.

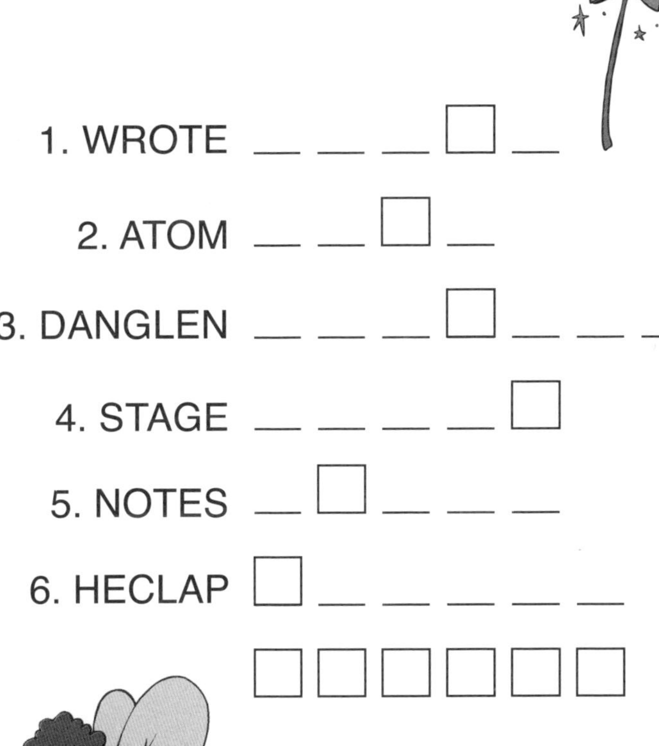

1. WROTE __ __ __ ☐ __

2. ATOM __ __ ☐ __

3. DANGLEN __ __ __ ☐ __ __ __

4. STAGE __ __ __ __ ☐

5. NOTES __ ☐ __ __ __

6. HECLAP ☐ __ __ __ __ __ __

☐ ☐ ☐ ☐ ☐ ☐

Answers on page 142.

Stop!

Which figure is the mirror image of the one in the box?

A.

B.

C.

D.

E.

 Answer on page 142.

Messy Room

Find the 12 differences in these 2 pictures.

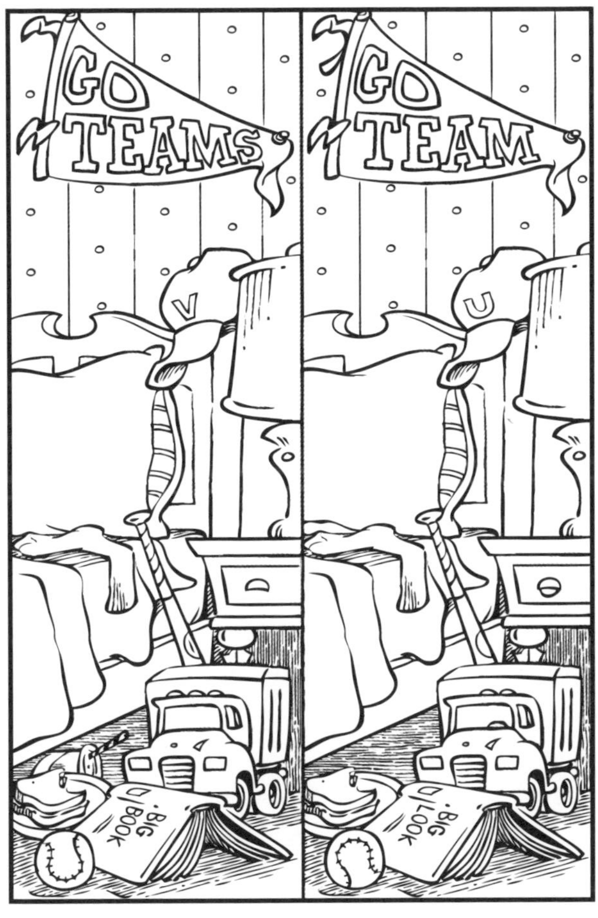

Answers on page 142.

Flippy Numbers

Below is an incorrect equation. Can you swap 2 of the number cards to get the correct equation?

Word Ladder

Can you change just one letter on each line to transform the top word to the bottom word? Don't change the order of the letters, and make sure you have a common English word at each step.

HEAT

____

____

____

COLD

Flower Growth

Which of these flowers has the longest stem?

Answer on page 143.

Keep On Truckin'

Which figure is the mirror image of the one in the box?

116

Answer on page 143.

Dot-to-Dot

Draw a line from consecutive numbers, starting at 1 and ending at 61, to reveal a froggy friend.

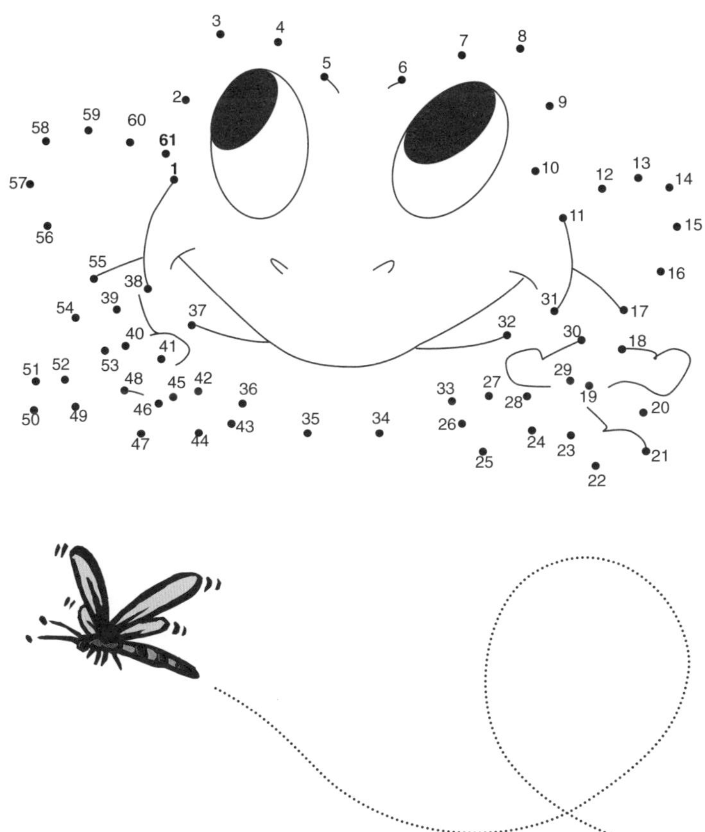

Answer on page 143.

Spoken Alphabet

Every word listed below is contained within the group of letters on the next page. Words can be found in a straight line horizontally, vertically, or diagonally. They may read either forward or backward.

ALFA	NOVEMBER
BRAVO	OSCAR
CHARLIE	PAPA
DELTA	QUEBEC
ECHO	ROMEO
FOXTROT	SIERRA
GOLF	TANGO
HOTEL	UNIFORM
INDIA	VICTOR
JULIET	WHISKEY
KILO	X-RAY
LIMA	YANKEE
MIKE	ZULU

```
X T T Z P J Z S I E R R A
R Y A N K E E I O U C F N
K C N N O S C A R N Z H T
Z E W Q G R E J L I Q G O
I B H U B O K A I F P V R
D E L T A M I L X O A F T
F U N O V E M B E R P R X
Z Q L E T O H V B M A F O
S F N Z E W H I S K E Y F
N C W L I P E C N O Q L O
C H A R L I E T A D O L A
W J D Q U M A O Q G I Y M
J E Z Q J B Z R Y K B A J
```

Answers on page 143.

Dog Park

There are 22 things wrong with this picture. Can you spot them all?

Answers on page 143.

Paper Fold

What household item's name is written on this folded paper?

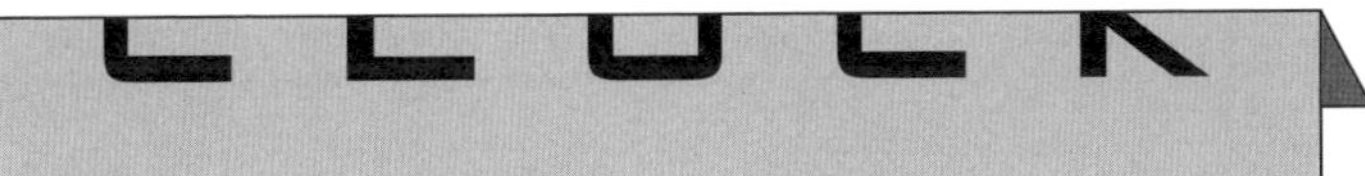

Word Ladder

Can you change just one letter on each line to transform the top word to the bottom word? Don't change the order of the letters, and make sure you have a common English word at each step.

ROCK

——

——

——

SAND

   Answers on page 144.

Across the Canyon

It's a treacherous path to get to the other side of this canyon! Can you make it across safely?

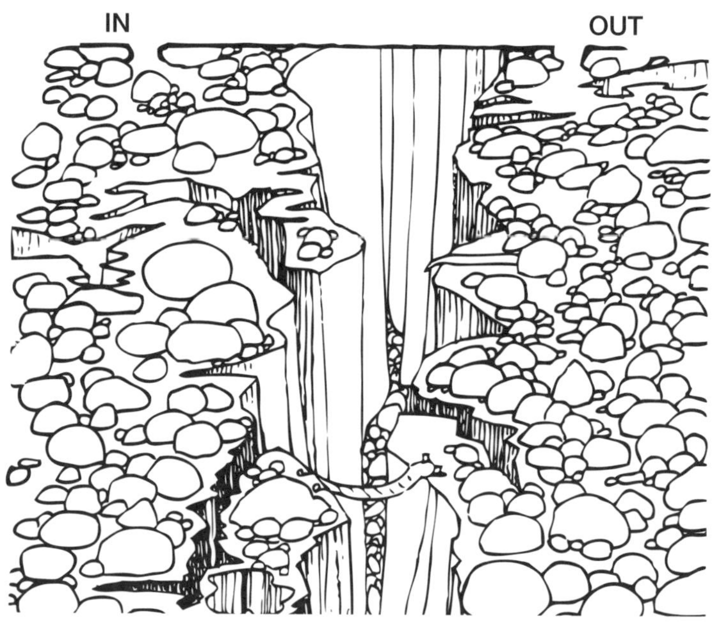

Answer on page 144.

Face Off

Can you spot the 2 identical faces?

 Answer on page 144.

Find the Blocks

Find the shapes below in the grid as many times as listed. Shapes cannot be flipped or turned.

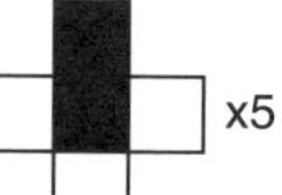

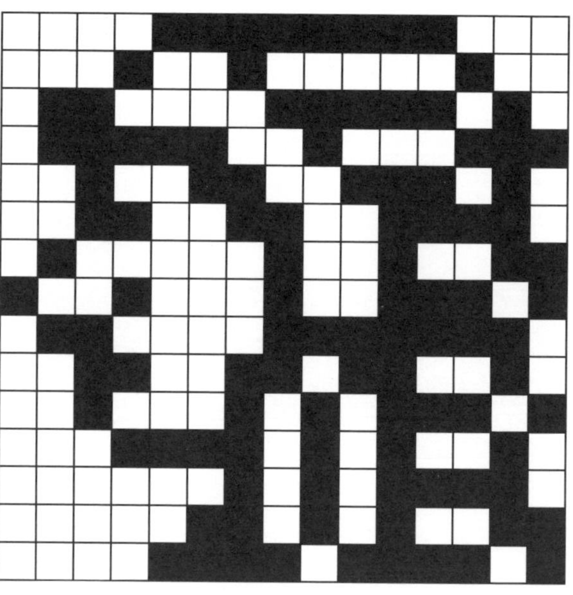

     Answers on page 144.

Pic-doku

The grid below is divided into 4 sections. Your job is to have each of the 4 fruits appear once in each section and in each row and column. Fill each square with the fruit's image or the letter that represents it. No item can repeat in any section, row, or column.

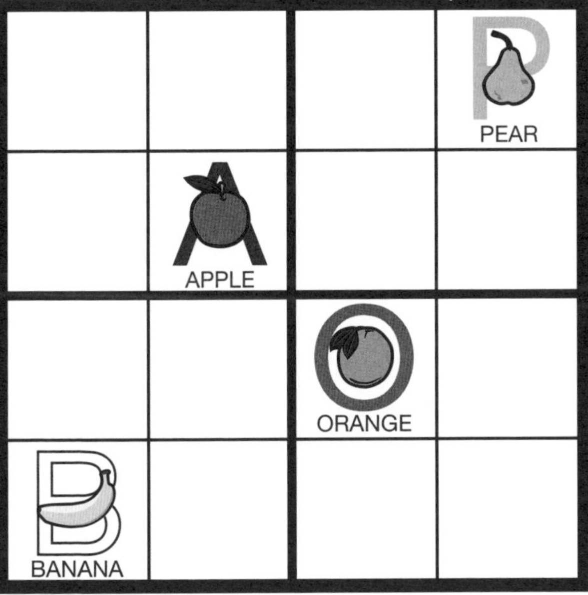

Answer on page 144.

Tangle

Several horseshoes have been laid on the table, one by one. Which one is on the bottom of the pile?

    Answer on page 144.

Scaffolding

Help this construction worker carefully climb down the scaffolding! You can travel underneath supports.

          Answer on page 144.

ANSWERS

Giraffe (page 6)

Fetch! (page 7)

Pic-doku (page 8)

Rhyme Time (page 9)

1. clam jam; 2. brown gown;
3. race place; 4. dime crime;
5. beach speech; 6. wet pet;
7. can ban; 8. neat street

Hen Party (page 10)

B. In A, it has a striped comb;
in C, it's missing its wattle

Have Your Cake (page 11)

Fit It (pages 12–13)

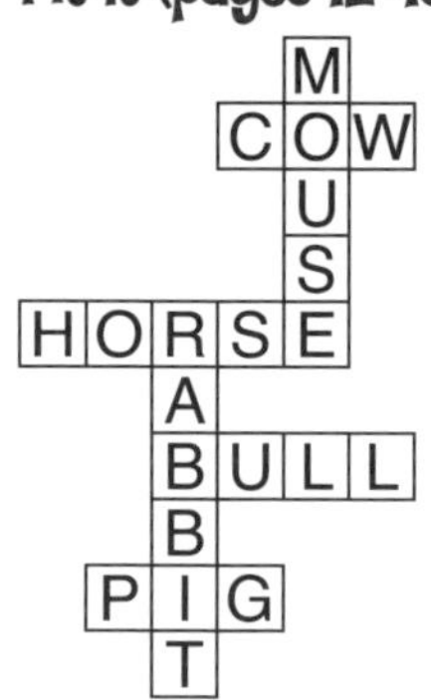

After Practice (page 14)

Flower Growth (page 15)

Dinner Party (pages 16–17)

Face Off (page 18)

Paper Fold (page 19)

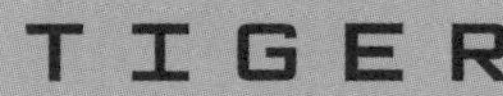

Word Ladder (page 19)

Answers may vary.
LID, lip, tip, TOP

Stop Signs (page 20)

Answers

Toy Box (page 21)

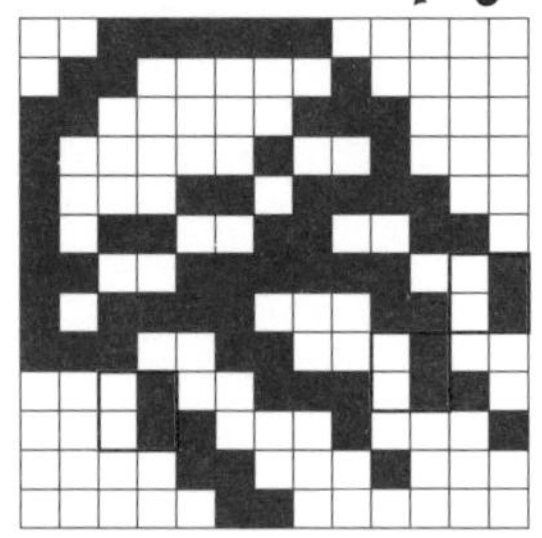

At the Zoo (page 22)

```
B J Z E B R A S K T W
B A T S L Y D R N E L
R J M L Z R K A S F L
T A A O A M H N E F R
N M G Z N P K X K A X
A T I U E K P M A R C
M L H L O X E P N I H
M K E Y R C R Y S G I
Y W A L L I R O G L M
L R N M H Z N L F K P
R J V R E G I T N K H
```

Find the Blocks (page 23)

1-2-3 (page 24)

```
3—1—2
1     3
2—3—1
    2
2—1—3
3     1
1—3—2
```

Egg Hunt (page 25)

Family Ties (page 26)

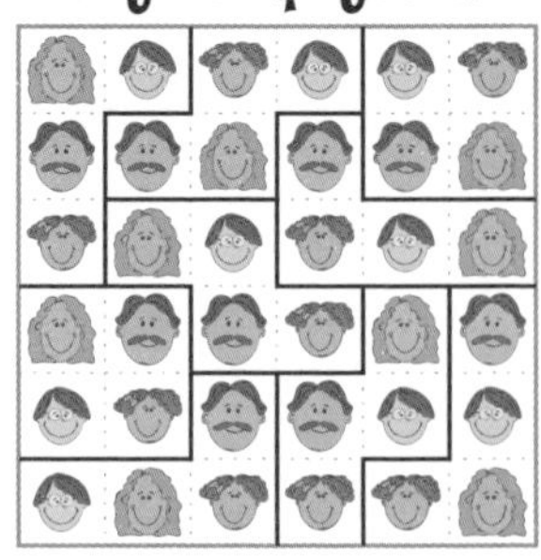

130

Hungry Fox (page 27)

Combo Crossword (pages 28-29)

Space Case (page 30)

Wagon Ride (page 31)

A. In B, the cart is missing its handle; in C, the boy's cap is striped; in D, there is a rabbit

Math (pages 32-33)

It's Magic (page 34)

Decoder (page 35)

Rail to the chief!

Answers

Staircase Crossword (pages 36-37)

W Is for Witch (page 38)

Wagon; warts; walrus; windows; wheels; webs; wood; wizard; wand; wreaths; witch

Flippy Numbers (page 39)

$$8 + 7 + 6 = 5 + 10$$

$$5 + 7 + 6 = 8 + 10$$

Chain Words (page 39)

Pic-doku (page 40)

Find the Blocks (page 41)

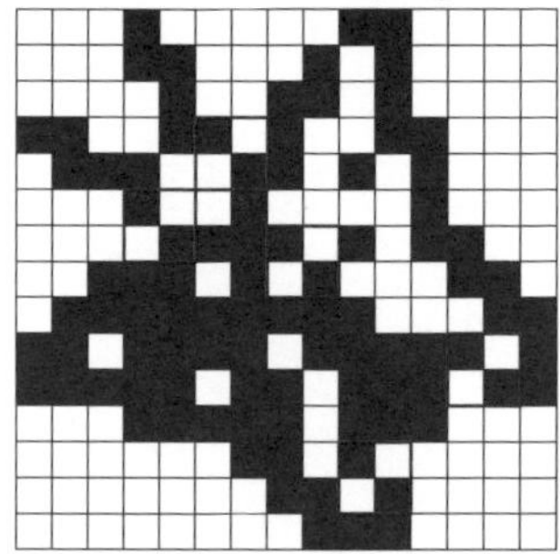

Snow Day (page 42)

B. In A, he has a black pom-pom; in C, there are 2 more snowballs

Wood Floor (page 43)

Anagrammar (page 44)

PURSE

Green Thumb (page 45)

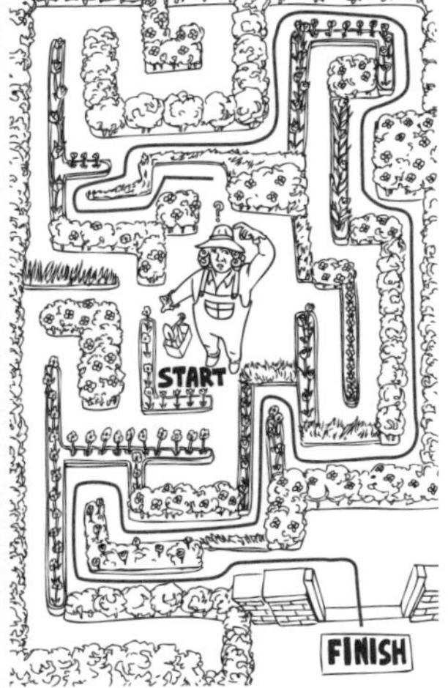

Boot Shopping (page 46)

Dog Walker (page 47)

Answers

Insects (pages 48-49)

Row Your Boat (pages 50-51)

Ribbit (page 52)

Flower Growth (page 53)

Squid on the High Seas (pages 54-55)

Picture Rhymes (page 56)

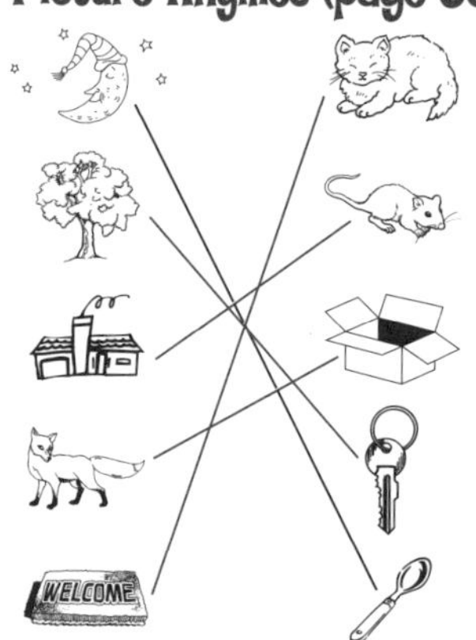

Night Light (page 57)

E. In A, there is an extra window; in B, the chimney has moved; in C, the railing is missing its uprights; in D, the ball at the top is gone

M Is for Marbles (page 58)

Marbles; monkey; monster mask; moon; moose; mountains; mouse; mushrooms; music

Zoo (page 59)

Face Off (page 60)

Dog Maze (page 61)

Letters on the Move (page 62)

POT, TOP

APE, PEA

STAR, RATS

CATS, CAST

TEN, NET

SLIP, LIPS

LAMP, PALM

SNAIL, NAILS

Answers

Find the Blocks (page 63)

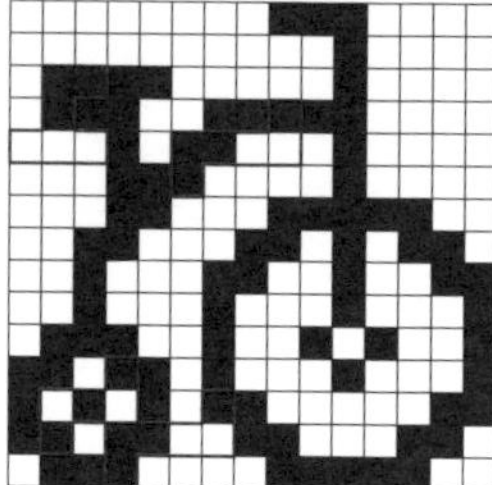

Picture-by-Number (page 64)

Tundra of T's (page 65)

Table; tambourine; teapot; teepee; telephone; telescope; tennis racket; tic-tac-toe; tiger; toad; toucan; train; trees; tulips; tunnel; turkey; turtle

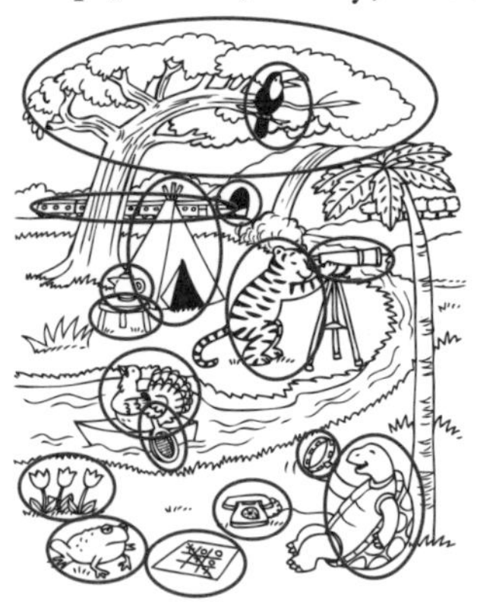

Rhyme Time (page 66)

1. bite might; 2. cow chow;
3. throne phone; 4. rich witch;
5. lizard blizzard; 6. flat hat;
7. freeze cheese; 8. moon tune;
9. dark park; 10. sandy candy

Polly Pirate (page 67)

State Your Name (pages 68-69)

Anagrammar (page 70)

INSECT

Black Hole (page 71)

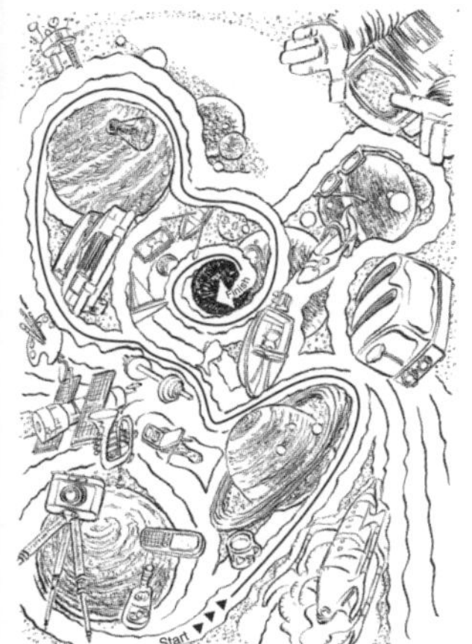

Sea World! (pages 72–73)

Pic-doku (page 74)

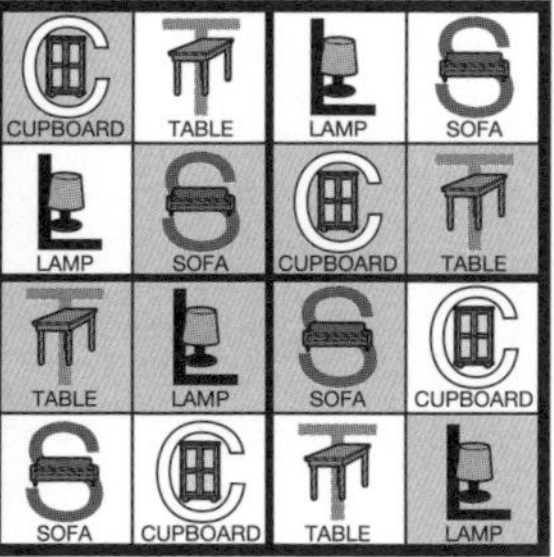

Rhyme Time (page 75)

1. dry spy; 2. bug jug;
3. grouch couch; 4. mean
queen; 5. pool rule; 6. blue
shoe; 7. mouse house;
8. mad lad

Family Ties (page 76)

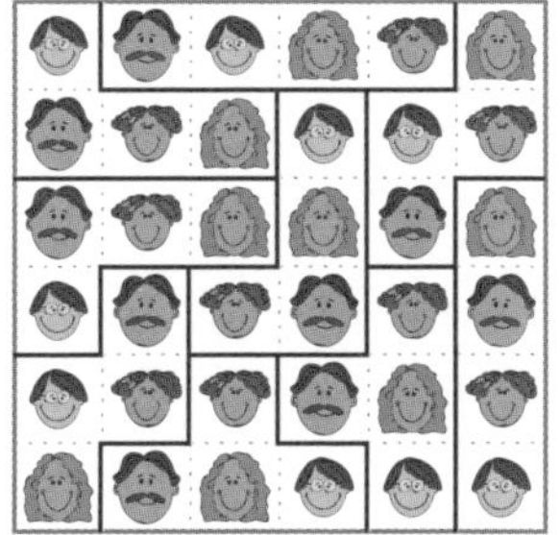

Polar-mobile (page 77)

Face Off (page 78)

Answers

Dot-to-Dot (page 79)

Art Class (page 80)

Paper Fold (page 81)

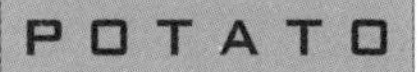

Chain Words (page 81)

Tricky Tomb (page 82)

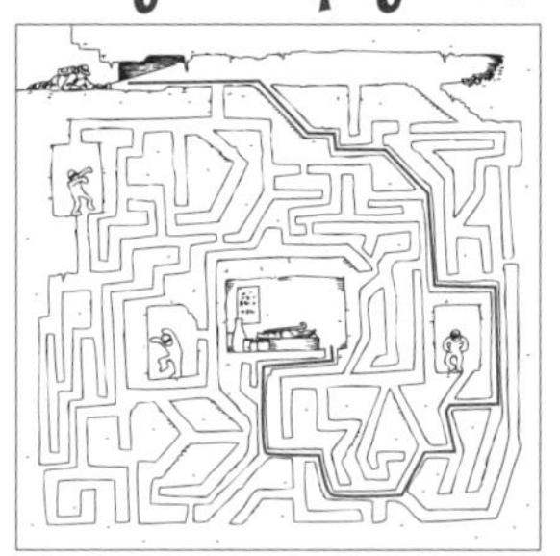

Flower Growth (page 83)

Robo Repair (page 84)

Farm Fiasco (page 85)

1. Square wheels on tractor;
2. glasses on tractor;
3. sheep on tractor; 4. flower in tractor exhaust; 5. elephant in stable; 6. farmer walking dog in pond; 7. bird flying upside down; 8. fish in window; 9. spider upside down in window; 10. cow on pig

Boo! (page 86)

A Rose Is a Rose (page 87)

A. In B, the rose is missing a leaf; in C, the stem is too short; in D, the rose has an extra leaf

Fruit Bowl (page 88)

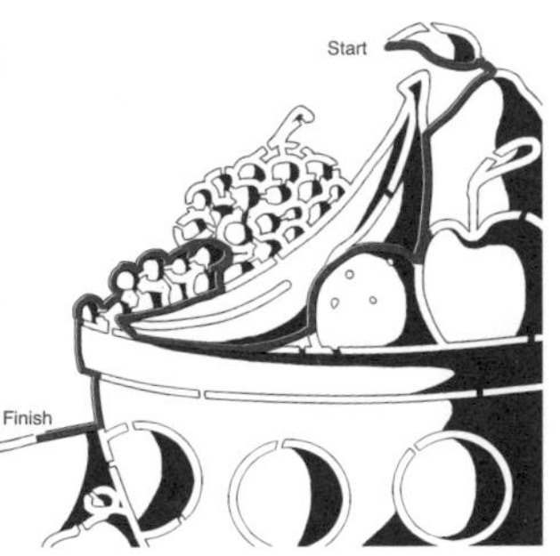

Airport (page 89)

1. Airplane flying upside down; 2. helicopter parked on its nose; 3. car too small for man; 4. elephant in control tower; 5. ship docked at terminal; 6. triangular wheels on firetruck; 7. woman's suitcase is floating; 8. man flying with suitcase; 9. man flying by umbrella; 10. airplane parked on top of control tower

Birds of a Feather (pages 90-91)

S	A	T		E	A	R	L
O	T	T	O		G	L	U	E
E	G	R	E	T		R	O	B	I	N
E	R	A		O	L	E		U	N	O
K	E	Y	S		A	D	A	M
		H	E	R	O	N
	S	H	A	G		T	H	E	E
T	R	I		S	E	A		O	R	E
E	A	G	L	E		Q	U	A	I	L
E	C	H	O		U	R	G	E
N	E	S	T		A	N	Y

Answers

Plenty of P's (page 92)

1. pail; 2. paint brush; 3. paint can; 4. painter; 5. pants;
6. parrot; 7. patch; 8. pears;
9. pen; 10. pencil; 11. pendant;
12. penny; 13. pepperoni;
14. pie; 15. piggy bank;
16. pilot; 17. pirate ; 18. pizza;
19. plane; 20. plant; 21. pony;
22. poster; 23. pushpin

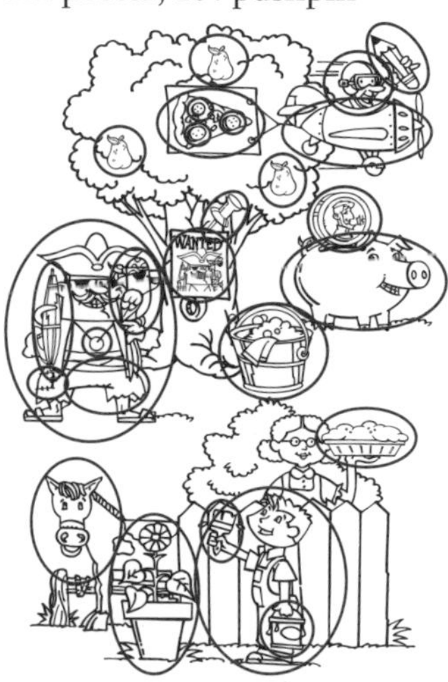

Go Fish (page 93)

There are 5 kinds of fish. There are more polka-dotted fish than striped fish. There is only 1 fish with black stripes.

Rhyme Time (pages 94-95)

1. big pig; 2. stuck truck;
3. marry Harry; 4. great bait;
5. spring sting; 6. deep sleep;
7. jester tester; 8. violet pilot;
9. nice mice; 10. white knight;
11. stable table; 12. choose shoes; 13. book crook; 14. long song; 15. fun run; 16. skip dip;
17. sells shells

Word Ladder (page 96)

Answers may vary.
WARM, worm, word, wood, wool, COOL

Paper Fold (page 96)

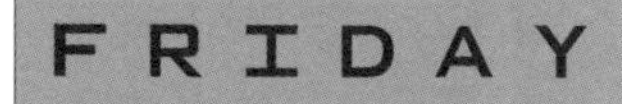

Fanfare (page 97)

C. In A, some flowers are missing; in B, a rib is missing; in D, there are too many flowers; in E, there are too many ribs

Pic-doku (page 98)

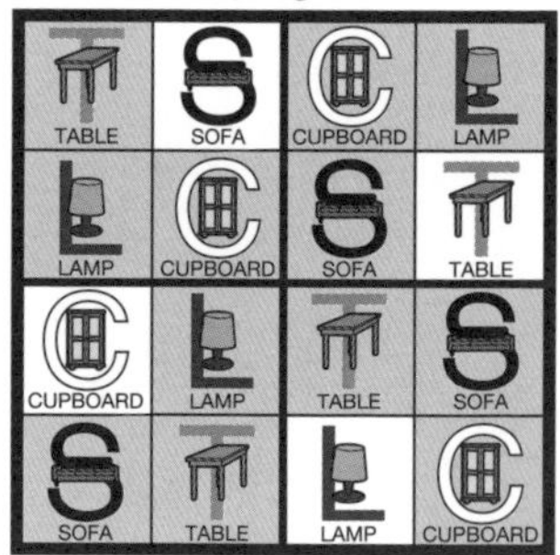

Monkeying Around (page 99)

Find the Blocks (page 100)

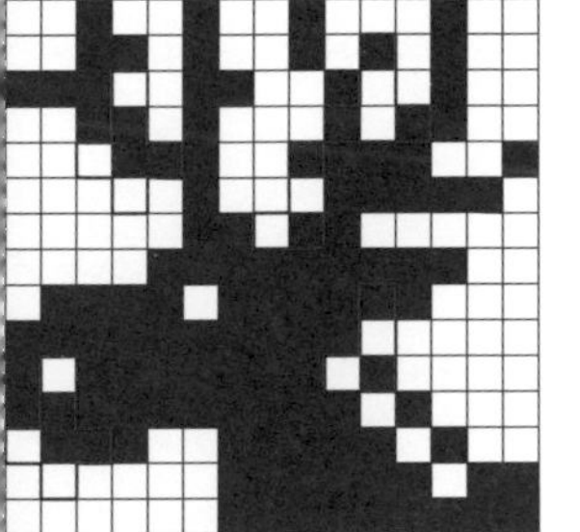

Tangle (page 101)

Fruit and Vegetable Stand (pages 102-103)

Corral the Cows (page 104)

Family Ties (page 105)

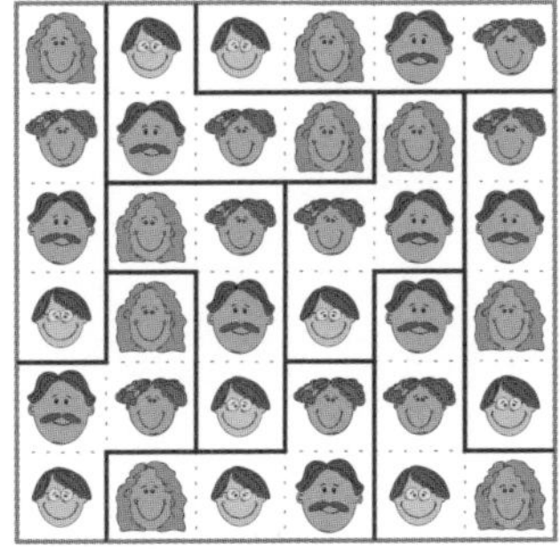

Answers

Picture-by-Number (page 106)

Jetpack! (page 107)

Pic-doku (page 108)

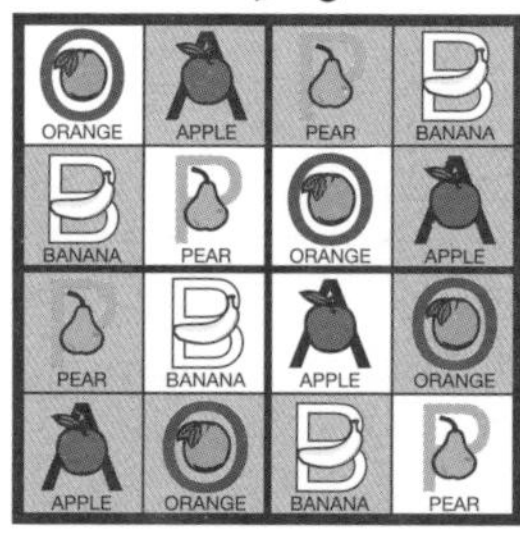

Recycling Day (page 109)

Riddle Scramble (pages 110–111)

T O W E R

M O A T

E N G L A N D

G A T E S

S T O N E

C H A P E L

C A S T L E

Stop! (page 112)

E. A is missing his whistle; B is missing his badge; C has a different glove; and D is missing a pants stripe

Messy Room (page 113)

Flippy Numbers (Page 114)

$$71 - 53 = 29$$

$$72 - 53 = 19$$

Word Ladder (page 114)

Answers may vary. HEAT, head, held, hold, COLD

Flower Growth (page 115)

Keep On Truckin' (page 116)

E. In A, there's a design on the door; in B, the hubs are missing; in C, some wheels are missing; in D, there is a design on the tank

Dot-to-Dot (page 117)

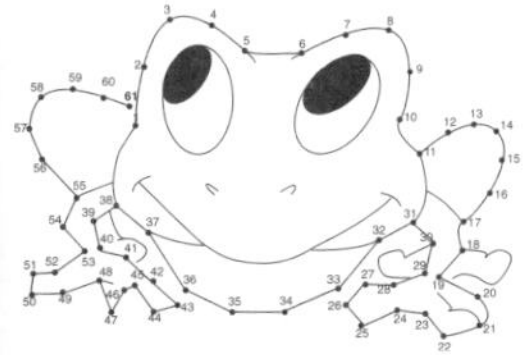

Spoken Alphabet (pages 118–119)

Dog Park (page 120)

1. face in tree; 2. rings on tree trunk; 3. man has dog head; 4. dog's head upside down; 5. dog has saddle; 6. dog wearing sandals; 7. cat in tree; 8. volcano erupting; 9. "NEWS" upside down; 10. man missing shoe; 11. tree trunk has face; 12. dog has flower on tail; 13. dog collar empty; 14. pizza slice in tree; 15. money in tree; 16. man has no neck; 17. man has feet for hands; 18. woman has robot head; 19. sign says "DAWG"; 20. dog has bowtie; 21. dog wearing cap; 22. bone is half wrench

Answers

Paper Fold (page 121)

Word Ladder (page 121)

Answers may vary. ROCK, sock, sack, sank, SAND

Across the Canyon (page 122)

Face Off (page 123)

Find the Blocks (page 124)

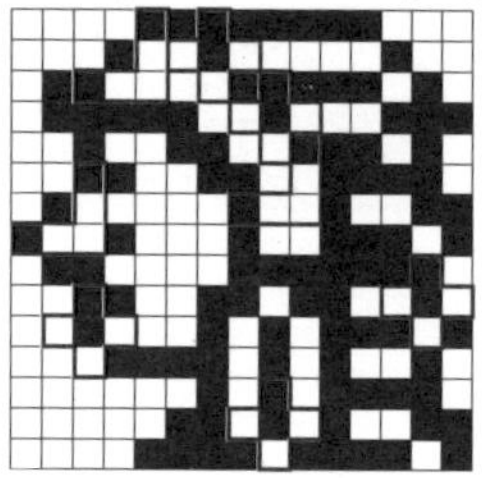

Pic-doku (page 125)

Tangle (page 126)

Scaffolding (page 127)

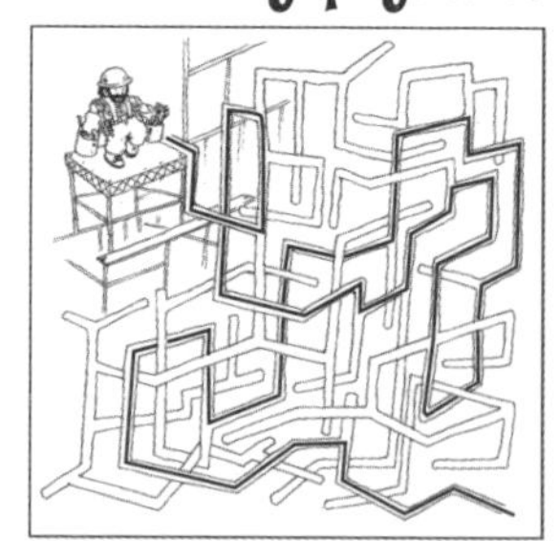